GH;

D0929592

Ulysses S. Grant

History Maker Bios

Susan Bivin Aller

⌐ LERNER PUBLICATIONS COMPANY • MINNEAPOLIS

For Jonathan Robin Aller, an All-American Boy in Paris

Illustrations by Tim Parlin

Text copyright © 2005 by Susan Bivin Aller
Illustrations copyright © 2005 by Lerner Publications Company

Lerner Publications Company
A division of Lerner Publishing Group
241 First Avenue North
Minneapolis, MN 55401 U.S.A.

Website address: www.lernerbooks.com

Library of Congress Cataloging-in-Publication Data

Aller, Susan Bivin.
   Ulysses S. Grant / by Susan Bivin Aller.
      p.   cm. — (History maker bios)
   Includes bibliographical references (p.   ) and index.
   ISBN: 0–8225–2438–4 (lib. bdg. : alk. paper)
   1. Grant, Ulysses S. (Ulysses Simpson), 1822–1885—Juvenile literature.
2. Presidents—United States—Biography—Juvenile literature. 3. Generals—
United States—Biography—Juvenile literature. 4. United States. Army—
Biography—Juvenile literature. I. Title. II. Series.
E672.A45 2005
973.8'2'092—dc22   2004004702

Manufactured in the United States of America
1 2 3 4 5 6 – JR – 10 09 08 07 06 05

TABLE OF CONTENTS

INTRODUCTION

Ulysses S. Grant never wanted to be in the army. Yet he became one of the most brilliant generals of all time. After attending the U.S. Military Academy at West Point, Grant served in the army for ten years. Then he left and became a farmer.

When the Civil War tore the North and South apart, Grant answered his country's call and returned to the army. He rose through the ranks to become general of all the Northern armies. Grant's leadership led to the defeat of the South and brought the South and North back together. After the war, a grateful nation elected Grant president of the United States.

This is his story.

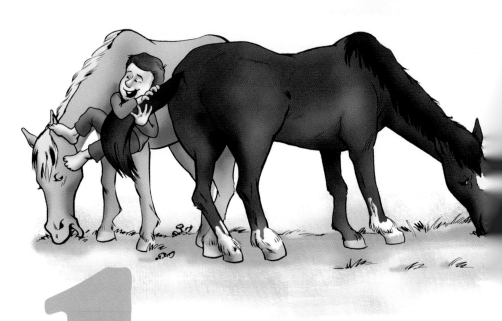

1

ALL-AMERICAN BOY

Hiram Ulysses Grant was born on April 27, 1822, in Point Pleasant, Ohio. He was the first of six children born to Jesse Root Grant and his wife Hannah Simpson Grant. His parents called their healthy, ten-pound baby Ulysses, after the strong Greek hero of the same name.

Ulysses's father was a tanner who made leather from animal hides. 'Lyss, as his family called him, hated the smelly, bloody business of tanning. But he loved anything to do with horses and farming. When he was tiny, he played around the teams of horses at the tannery. Sometimes he grabbed their tails and swung from them. His parents didn't worry. "Horses seem to understand Ulysses," his mother said.

Ulysses Grant was born in this house in Ohio.

By the time 'Lyss was eight, his father let him drive the horses that pulled wagonloads of firewood and bark used for tanning. By the age of eleven, 'Lyss could do almost as much farmwork as a grown man. He had an amazing ability to control horses. Farmers brought colts for him to train. A crowd often gathered to watch him work.

At seventeen, Ulysses was accepted into the U.S. Military Academy at West Point. He would be a cadet, a student training to be an officer in the military. Jesse Grant wanted the best education possible for his eldest son. At West Point, the government would pay for it.

The U.S. Military Academy at West Point, New York (CENTER) was founded in 1802.

Ulysses (CENTER) salutes General Winfield Scott at West Point.

When Ulysses got to West Point, he found that the school had his name wrong on the list of new cadets. Instead of "Hiram Ulysses Grant," he was "Ulysses Simpson Grant." In spite of his attempts to change it, the name stuck.

Ulysses was well liked by the other cadets. He was honest and fair and didn't use bad language. "I never learned to swear," he said. "I have noticed that swearing helps to rouse a man's anger."

Ulysses was small for his age and didn't like rough sports. He often slipped away to read instead of study. His grades weren't very good, except in art and horsemanship.

Ulysses painted "Trading with Indians" (BELOW) while he was a West Point cadet.

A Record Jump

Ulysses set one record at West Point—in horse jumping. During graduation, the cadets showed how they could ride their horses. Cadet Grant and his horse York were called on to jump over a bar that was more than six feet high. Ulysses and his horse thundered down the riding hall. They sailed over the jump "as if man and beast were welded together." No one beat their record jump for twenty-five years.

Ulysses finished school in 1843. West Point cadets like Ulysses had a job to do after they finished school. They had to serve one year in the army.

The army put Ulysses in a unit at Jefferson Barracks, near Saint Louis, Missouri. After that, he planned to leave the army and become a math teacher.

Soon there were other things on 'Lyss's mind besides army duties. In February 1843, he met seventeen-year-old Julia Dent. Julia was the sister of 'Lyss's West Point roommate, Fred Dent. After meeting her, Ulysses was a regular caller at the Dents' house. He loved taking the beautiful, intelligent Julia to parties.

In May 1844, Ulysses's unit was ordered to travel south to the border between Louisiana and Texas. It was then that Ulysses realized he was in love with Julia. The couple became engaged. Two days later, Ulysses left for Texas.

2 "Sorry That I Had Enlisted"

Second Lieutenant Grant joined his army unit in June 1844. He wrote home: "I have a small tent that the rain runs through. . . . The swamps are full of alligators, and the wood full of red bugs and ticks."

Grant's regiment had been sent to help protect Americans living in Texas. Texas had belonged to Mexico, but it broke away. In 1845, Texas became part of the United States. About this time, the United States and Mexico were arguing about who owned the land around southern Texas. It looked as if the two countries might go to war over it.

Grant felt it would be a very unjust war. He felt that the United States just wanted to go to war to take Mexican land. But he was a good soldier, and he followed his orders. The orders came from Grant's commander, General Zachary Taylor. Grant admired "Old Rough-and-Ready" Taylor.

General Zachary Taylor stands beside his horse.

Taylor wasn't a show-off. Instead of wearing his general's uniform, he often wore denim pants with a long linen coat and a straw hat. He put his men at ease, and they became very loyal to him. He spoke few words, but when he did, his orders were clear. He remained calm in the face of danger.

In May 1846, Mexican soldiers fired on the Americans, and the war began. Grant, who was twenty-four, had never heard an enemy gun before. "I felt sorry that I had enlisted [joined the army]," he wrote. Grant's unit was in charge of moving the supplies, setting up camp, and providing food and equipment for the men, horses, and mules.

Fighting between the Mexicans and the Americans started in Mexico.

The United States won the war and gained much land in the Southwest and the West. Grant hurried back to Saint Louis. He and his beloved Julia were married in August 1848.

Grant decided to stay in the army. He took his bride with him to his new assignment near Detroit. Their first child, Frederick, was born there in 1850.

Grant was twenty-six years old when he married Julia. She was twenty-two.

After the Mexican War (1846–1848) ended, the army sent Grant to Fort Vancouver in the Oregon Territory on the northwestern frontier.

In 1852, Grant's army unit was ordered west, to Fort Vancouver in the Oregon Territory. Thousands of settlers and miners had rushed to the West Coast after gold was found there. The army's job was to protect them. Grant wanted to take Julia with him, but she was expecting another baby and couldn't make the long, difficult journey.

Without Julia, Grant was lonely and unhappy. Julia's first letter didn't reach him for several months. She told him the new baby had been born. She had named him Ulysses S. Grant Jr. Grant longed to be near his family.

In May 1854, Grant left the army. He returned home with no money. He was glad to be with his family again. Julia's father gave them some farmland. On it, Grant built a log house for them to live in.

In 1858, Grant suffered a yearlong illness. It may have been malaria. The daily fever and chills made it difficult for him to work on the farm. When the farm failed, he took other jobs. One winter, he put on his faded old army coat and carried firewood in a wagon to sell in Saint Louis. He was so poor he even sold his gold watch so his family could have money to celebrate Christmas.

Finally, in 1860, Grant moved his family to Galena, Illinois. He needed work. His father's tanning business had grown to more than fifty workers. Ulysses went to work as a clerk in one of the company stores.

3 GENERAL GRANT

Ulysses and Julia were happy to be together. They had four children: Frederick, Ulysses S. Jr., Ellen, and Jesse. If it hadn't been for the outbreak of the Civil War the next year, Ulysses Grant might have stayed in Galena, Illinois, for the rest of his life. But a war between the North and the South was coming.

For years, the United States had struggled with the subject of slavery. In the South, slaves did much of the physical work for rich landowners. Their owners could buy and sell them like any other property. As new states joined the United States, Southerners wanted them to allow slavery too. But in the North, many people believed it was wrong for one man to own another. They especially wanted new states to ban slavery.

GRANT AND SLAVERY

Julia's father gave the Grants a young slave named William Jones to help with the farmwork. Grant could have used his help on the farm. He even could have sold Jones for a thousand dollars or more and used the money to pay his bills. Instead, Grant gave Jones his freedom. Grant hated slavery. He didn't believe one man should own another.

Abraham Lincoln

When Abraham Lincoln was elected president in 1860, Southerners were afraid he would force them to free their slaves. First, South Carolina left, or seceded, from the United States. More Southern states followed. They formed their own country and allowed slavery. They called their country the Confederate States of America and elected Jefferson Davis president. The people who wanted the country to stay together called the United States the Union. They said secession was against the laws of the United States. It had to be stopped.

The first shots of the Civil War were fired at Fort Sumter in South Carolina on April 12, 1861. Confederate soldiers fired the first shot. A few days later, President Abraham Lincoln called for seventy-five thousand men to join the Union army for three months. Ulysses Grant was eager to serve his country. He hurried to the Galena courthouse as soon as he heard the call for soldiers.

Grant was calm and steady. He wrote orders so clearly that there was no doubt about what he wanted his men to do. He got the job done without complaining or making excuses.

Grant was one of the few people in Galena with military experience. He took charge of training the town's soldiers.

Grant liked to stay close to the battlefield. He watched the action with these field glasses.

President Lincoln needed men like Grant to lead the Union armies. In May 1861, Lincoln made Grant a brigadier general and gave him command of Union troops on the Mississippi River.

In 1861, Southern soldiers had been winning most of the battles. But Grant quickly changed that. In February 1862, he captured two important Confederate forts that guarded the Tennessee and Cumberland rivers. Fort Henry and Fort Donelson were the North's first major victories of the war.

General Simon Bolivar Buckner was one of the Confederate leaders who surrendered to Grant at Fort Donelson in Tennessee.

When the Confederate generals saw that they would lose, they wrote to Grant. They asked what would happen to them if they stopped fighting. They wanted to know the terms of surrender. "No terms," Grant wrote. "No terms except unconditional and immediate surrender can be accepted." Grant demanded that they give up without trying to bargain with him.

But Grant showed respect for the Southern soldiers. He let them take their guns and horses home with them. They had already lost the battle. Grant didn't want to make life even more difficult for them by taking away everything they owned.

Two months later, Grant's army fought Confederates near the Shiloh meeting house at Pittsburg Landing, Tennessee. It was one of the bloodiest battles of the war. More than twenty-three thousand men of the North and South died. Grant was criticized for letting so many men be killed. But President Lincoln defended Grant. "I can't spare this man," he said. "He fights."

More than twenty-three thousand men died in the Battle of Shiloh in 1862.

Then Lincoln chose Grant to lead the attack against Vicksburg, Mississippi. Vicksburg was the most important Confederate city on the Mississippi River. If the North captured Vicksburg, it could control the river and divide the Confederacy in half. Grant knew it would be difficult. But once he decided to do something, he never turned back or stopped until he reached his goal.

FAMILY VISITS

Julia Grant and other officers' wives often stayed with their husbands between battles. Grant was happiest when Julia and their children were near. When Grant's oldest son, Fred, was only eleven years old, he traveled alone with his father for several months. A year later, Fred stayed with Grant through the long battle of Vicksburg.

Grant's forces surrounded Vicksburg and made sure no food or other supplies were able to get into the city. People living in the city suffered terribly from disease and lack of food.

Finally, the Confederate troops in Vicksburg were ready to surrender. The Confederate general asked Grant for his terms. Again, Grant said no terms, only unconditional surrender.

The army of thirty-one thousand men surrendered to Grant on July 4, 1863. Grant's army took over the city. The Union could then send men and supplies farther down the Mississippi River. Union troops could fight Confederate soldiers in the heart of the South. People began saying that the "U. S." in Grant's name stood for "Unconditional Surrender."

President Lincoln praised Grant. "Grant is my man," he said. "And I am his the rest of the war."

4 NO BACKWARD STEPS

Grant knew the fall of Vicksburg
marked the beginning of the end
for the Confederacy. But there was much
hard fighting to be done before the South
finally surrendered. Grant went on to
Chattanooga, Tennessee, in November
1863. He rescued the Union army that the
Confederate troops had trapped there.

President Lincoln invited Grant to Washington to receive a gold medal. Lincoln made Grant the lieutenant general in charge of all the Union armies. Grant, at the age of forty-one, certainly didn't look like a great commander. He looked tired and rumpled. He didn't even dress like an army officer.

Grant usually wore an ordinary soldier's uniform, with his general's stars pinned on the shoulders. He sometimes tucked his pants' legs into his boots and wore a wide-brimmed, soft hat.

Grant (STANDING, WEARING A WIDE-BRIMMED HAT) preferred a more casual uniform in the field.

Grant used this lantern to study maps and to plan battles long after dark.

Grant's military skill set him apart from all the other officers. One of his special talents was that he could look at a map and see the land, trees, and roads in his mind. Then he could picture how soldiers would be arranged over hundreds of miles and how they could move and fight in that setting.

As soon as he was in charge of all the Union armies, he began to think about a grand plan to win the war. His idea was to move all the Union armies at the same time. They would hammer the Confederate armies without stopping until the Southerners had to surrender.

The armies began their move in May 1864. Grant himself went with General George Meade and the Army of the Potomac to chase General Robert E. Lee's army. Both Grant and Lee were brilliant military leaders. But Grant and the North had far more men and supplies than the South did.

"Wherever Lee goes, there you will go also," Grant told Meade. Lee headed for the Wilderness, an area of northern Virginia covered by dense forests and underbrush.

The fierce fighting lasted two days. Neither side had won, but both sides had lost thousands of men.

Generals Grant and Meade study a map before the Wilderness battle.

Grant (CENTER, ON A HORSE) leads his army to Spotsylvania. A newspaper reporter made this drawing. Most Civil War reporters did not have cameras.

Grant wanted to force Lee to fight in the open. He marched his army to a small town called Spotsylvania. Lee would have to pass that way, and Grant planned a surprise attack.

The armies were locked in battle at Spotsylvania for nearly two weeks. Grant said he would "fight it out on this line if it takes all summer. . . . I shall take no backward steps." Grant pushed Lee and his army farther and farther south toward Richmond, the Confederate capitol.

The fighting continued for almost a year. Finally, Lee's hungry, worn-out army was trapped by Union troops. On April 9, 1865, Grant met Lee at Appomattox Court House, Virginia. Grant wrote out the terms of surrender. He wrote quickly and in his usual clear style "so that there could be no mistaking it."

Grant let the defeated Southerners keep their guns and horses and mules. He did not take them prisoner. They could go home and return to their private lives.

Grant generously let Lee (CENTER FRONT) leave Appomattox on his horse.

Grant returned to Washington, D.C., on April 13. He went to army headquarters and began giving orders for ending the war. That night, he and President Lincoln rode through the city. They saw a grand display of lighted buildings in celebration of Lee's surrender. They were cheered at every corner.

The next day, Grant accepted an invitation to attend a play at Ford's Theatre with President and Mrs. Lincoln. But Julia wanted to go to see the children in New Jersey. Grant apologized to the president and left Washington by train.

Inside Ford's Theatre, the U.S. president's private box was as elegant as a room in the White House.

When the train stopped in Philadelphia, a message was handed to Grant. It read: "The President was assassinated at Ford's Theatre at 10:30 tonight and cannot live." A Southerner had shot Lincoln. He died the next day.

"It was the darkest day of my life," Grant told a reporter. Grant personally made arrangements for Lincoln's funeral. The coffin was covered with a black cloth and placed on a raised platform in the East Room of the White House. Throughout the funeral service, General Ulysses S. Grant stood alone at the head of the coffin, often weeping.

Assassination Attempt

Someone also tried to kill Grant that same night. While he and Julia were on the train, a man tried to force his way into their car. A note was later found describing the plot to kill Grant.

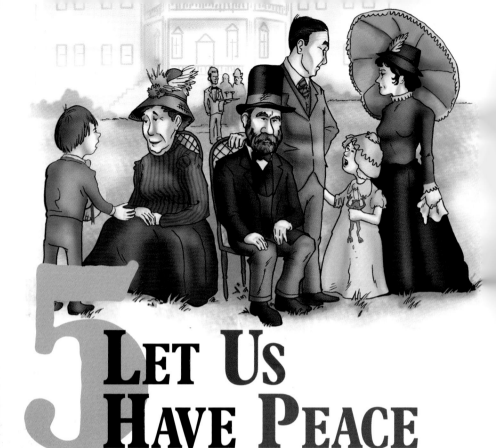

5 LET US HAVE PEACE

Grant worked hard to help bring the Southern states peacefully back into the union. When Lincoln died, Vice President Andrew Johnson became president. Grant did not always agree with Johnson. As the election drew near in 1868, Grant became the popular choice for president. He was the war hero who had saved the nation. Grant's campaign slogan was Let Us Have Peace. He easily won the election. At the age of forty-six, he was the youngest president ever elected.

He and Julia and their children were happy in the White House. Julia had it completely redecorated and held weekly parties in its sparkling rooms.

Jesse (LEFT) and Ellen, called Nellie (RIGHT), pose with their mother Julia for a photo.

Grant took care of many important issues during his presidency. Slavery had ended, and he worked to give the former slaves their full rights as free men. He ended the wars against Native American tribes on the Great Plains. Even so, he was blamed for many of the country's problems. But he was so popular with the people that he was elected to a second term in 1872.

The next four years were even more difficult than the first. There was a lot of corruption, or wrongdoing, in the government, and many people complained about it.

President Grant presented this medal (BOTH SIDES SHOWN) to Chief Joseph of the Nez Perce in 1871.

There was never any hint that Grant did anything dishonest, but the many problems made him look like a failure. "I did not want the presidency," he said. He also said he was sorry he left the army to become president.

When Grant's term as president ended in 1876, he and Julia took a two-year trip around the world. Wherever they went, Grant was greeted as the general who had won the Civil War.

Julia and Grant (FRONT ROW, SEATED SECOND AND THIRD FROM THE LEFT) visited the Temple of Amon-Ra at Karnak, Egypt, in 1876.

After they returned to the United States, the Grants lived in New York City. Then a crooked banker cheated Grant out of all his money. That same summer, Grant found he was suffering from throat cancer. He needed money, so he began to write about the Civil War for *Century* magazine. The magazine paid him well.

MARK TWAIN, FAMILY FRIEND

The writer Mark Twain was a friend of Grant. He wanted to help Grant pay off his debts and have some money to leave his wife and family. So Twain offered to have his publishing company print Grant's book. He gave Grant's family most of the money from sales of the book. Thousands of copies of the book were sold, and Grant's family earned nearly $450,000.

He wrote quickly and in a strong, clear style. His stories of the war were fascinating. Readers wanted more. *Century*'s editors asked him to write the story of his life.

Grant spent the last months of his life writing this book. He died on July 23, 1885, just a few days after finishing it. *Personal Memoirs of U.S. Grant* stands as one of the greatest books about war ever written.

Grant was in a lot of pain in the last months of his life, but he kept writing.

The funeral march for Grant held in New York reminded people of Lincoln's funeral.

Ulysses S. Grant's funeral parade in New York City was seven miles long. More than sixty thousand marchers took part, and more than a million people watched.

After Grant's death, people raised money to build a tomb fit for a hero. The site chosen was a high point in Riverside Park in New York City, overlooking the Hudson River.

In 1892, the grand monument known as Grant's Tomb was finished. Inside the building are two large coffins of polished red stone. They are the final resting places of Ulysses S. Grant and his wife, Julia, who died in 1902.

Robert E. Lee, the general Grant defeated in the Civil War, said of him, "I have carefully searched the military records of both ancient and modern history and have never found Grant's superior as a general. I doubt if his superior can be found in all history."

Grant's Tomb is the largest structure of its kind in North America.

TIMELINE

ULYSSES GRANT
WAS BORN ON
APRIL 27, 1822.

In the year . . .

1839 Ulysses Grant entered the U.S. Military Academy at West Point.

1843 he graduated from West Point.

1844 he and his army unit were ordered to the Texas border.

Age 22

1846 the Mexican War began.

1848 he married Julia Dent in August.

Age 26

1852 he was stationed at Fort Vancouver, Oregon Territory.

1854 he resigned from the army and tried farming.

1860 he and his family moved to Galena, Illinois. he worked as a clerk in the family store. Abraham Lincoln was elected president.

1861 the Civil War began. Lincoln gave Grant command of Union troops in the West.

Age 39

1862 Grant captured Forts Henry and Donelson. he led the Union army at the Battle of Shiloh.

1863 Vicksburg surrendered to Grant's forces. his troops won the Battle of Chattanooga, Tennessee.

1864 he was named general of all the Union armies.

1865 General Lee surrendered to Grant on April 9. President Lincoln was shot on April 14.

1868 Grant was elected president.

Age 46

1872 he was reelected to the presidency.

1876 he and Julia traveled around the world.

1885 Grant died in New York City on July 23.

Age 63

GRANT'S HORSES

Grant's love for horses continued throughout his life. He had a number of fine horses during the war, but his favorite was Cincinnati (*pictured below*). Grant rode him to receive Lee's surrender at Appomattox. President Lincoln was also an expert horseman. Whenever he visited Grant on the battlefield, Grant let him ride Cincinnati. But few other men were ever allowed to do that.

Further Reading

NONFICTION

Collins, David R. *Mark T-W-A-I-N: A Story about Samuel Clemens.* Minneapolis: Carolrhoda Books, Inc., 1994. This book tells of the life of the writer and humorist who was a friend of Ulysses Grant in later years.

Ransom, Candice. *Children of the Civil War.* Minneapolis: Carolrhoda Books, Inc., 1998. Photos and text capture the lives of children during the war, as soldiers, at home, in school, and those made homeless by the war.

Ransom, Candice. *Robert E. Lee.* Minneapolis: Lerner Publications Company, 2005. Read about Grant's foe, Confederate general Robert E. Lee, in this History Maker Biography.

Ransom, Candice. *Willie McLean and the Civil War Surrender.* Minneapolis: Carolrhoda Books, Inc, 2005. Young Willie McLean's house becomes the site of the famous meeting between Grant and General Robert E. Lee.

Schott, Jane A. *Abraham Lincoln.* Minneapolis: Lerner Publications Company, 2002. A History Maker Biography of the Civil War president from his childhood in a log cabin to his life in the White House.

FICTION

Osborne, Mary Pope. *After the Rain: Virginia's Civil War Diary, Book Two.* New York: Scholastic, 2002. A ten-year-old girl tells of her time in Washington, D.C., at the end of the war, when Lincoln is assassinated.

Polacco, Patricia. *Pink and Say.* New York: Philomel, 1994. Two teenaged Union soldiers, one white and one black, learn to trust each other while under fire and as Confederate prisoners.

WEBSITES

The Ulysses S. Grant Network
http://www.css.edu/usgrant Visitors to this site can be connected to other Grant websites and organizations. It also contains a fairly extensive biography of Grant and a selection of photographs.

SELECT BIBLIOGRAPHY

Bedwell, Randall, ed. *May I Quote You, General Grant?* Nashville: Cumberland House, 1998.

Cowan, Mary Morton. "What Kind of a General Was He?" *Cobblestone,* October 1995, 48.

Grant, Julia Dent. *The Personal Memoirs of Julia Dent Grant (Mrs. Ulysses S. Grant).* New York: G. P. Putnam's Sons, 1975.

Grant, Ulysses S. *Personal Memoirs of U. S. Grant.* 1885. Reprint, New York: Penguin Books, 1999.

Smith, Jean Edward. *Grant.* New York: Simon and Schuster, 2001.

INDEX

Acknowledgments

For photographs and artwork: The images in this book are used with the permission of: National Archives, p. 4; Library of Congress, pp. 7 (LC-USZ62-23789), 8 (LC-USZC2-1877), 9 (LC-USZC4-1866), 14 (LC-USZ62-7559), 15 (LC-USZ62-1270), 17 (LC-USZ61-496), 21 (LC-USZ62-4377), 22 (LC-USZC4-1866), 24 (LC-DIG-cwpb-07434), 25 (LC-USZ62-3581), 31 (LC-DIG-cwpb-01191), 32 (LC-USZC4-10096), 33 (LC-USZ62-11095), 34 (LC-DIG-cwpb-02961); 37 (LC-DIG-cwpbh-00519), 39 (LC-USZ62-092457), 41 (LC-USZ62-7607), 42 (LC-USZC4-1814), 45 (LC-USZ62-101396), © West Point Museum Art Collection, United States Military Academy, pp. 10, 23, 30; Hulton|Archive by Getty Images, p. 16; U.S. Signal Corps, National Archives, p. 29; MSCUA, University of Washington Libraries, p. 38 (left [NA955], right [NA944]); Independent Picture Service, p. 43; front and back covers: West Point Museum Art Collection, United States Military Academy.
For quoted material: pp. 7, 11, 13, 24, 25, 27, 32, 35, Jean Edward Smith, *Grant,* (New York: Simon and Schuster, 2001); pp. 10, 39, Randall Bedwell, ed., *May I Quote You, General Grant?* (Nashville: Cumberland House, 1998); pp. 15, 31, 32, 33, Ulysses S. Grant, *Personal Memoirs of U. S. Grant* (1885; repr., New York: Penguin Books, 1999); p. 43, Mary Morton Cowan, "What Kind of General Was He?" *Cobblestone,* October 1995, 48.